Johann Baptist Cramer

Eighty-Four Celebrated Studies for the Pianoforte

ISBN/EAN: 9783744783637

Printed in Europe, USA, Canada, Australia, Japan

Cover: Foto ©Thomas Meinert / pixelio.de

More available books at **www.hansebooks.com**

Schirmer's Library of Musical Classics

Vols. 142–145

Johann Baptist Cramer

EIGHTY-FOUR CELEBRATED STUDIES

FOR THE

PIANOFORTE

IN FOUR BOOKS

Book I. Studies 1–21
Book II. Studies 22–42
Book III. Studies 43–63
Book IV. Studies 64–84

BOOK I. CONTAINS A BIOGRAPHICAL SKETCH OF THE AUTHOR
BY
DR. THEO. BAKER

NEW YORK : G. SCHIRMER
BOSTON : BOSTON MUSIC CO.
1894

Studies.

Book II.

J. B. CRAMER.

Allegro moderato. (♩ = 144.)

22.

pp *cresc.* *f* *ff* *pp* *cresc.* *f* *ff* *pp* *cresc.*

scen
do
f
dim.
cresc.
ff
dimin.

Con brio. (♪ = 152.)
23.
dimin.

ff
fz
dim.
ff
ff
fz
fz
cresc.
dim.
mf
cresc.
dim.

Con moto. (♩= 92.)
24.
pp
f
dim.
pp
cresc.
f
dim.
pp
cresc.

11722

Andante cantabile sostenuto. (♩= 66.)
25.
dolce
Il basso sempre legato
cresc.
p
mf
f

mf
cresc.
rf
dimin.
dolce

Moderato. (♩. = 60.)
26.
p
cresc.
f
dimin.
sfz
dimin.
f
dimin.

p
dim.
pp
cresc.
f
dim.
p
pp

Vivacissimo. (𝅗𝅥 = 152.)

sempre legato.

27.

mf

dim.

f

fz

fz

cresc.
decresc.

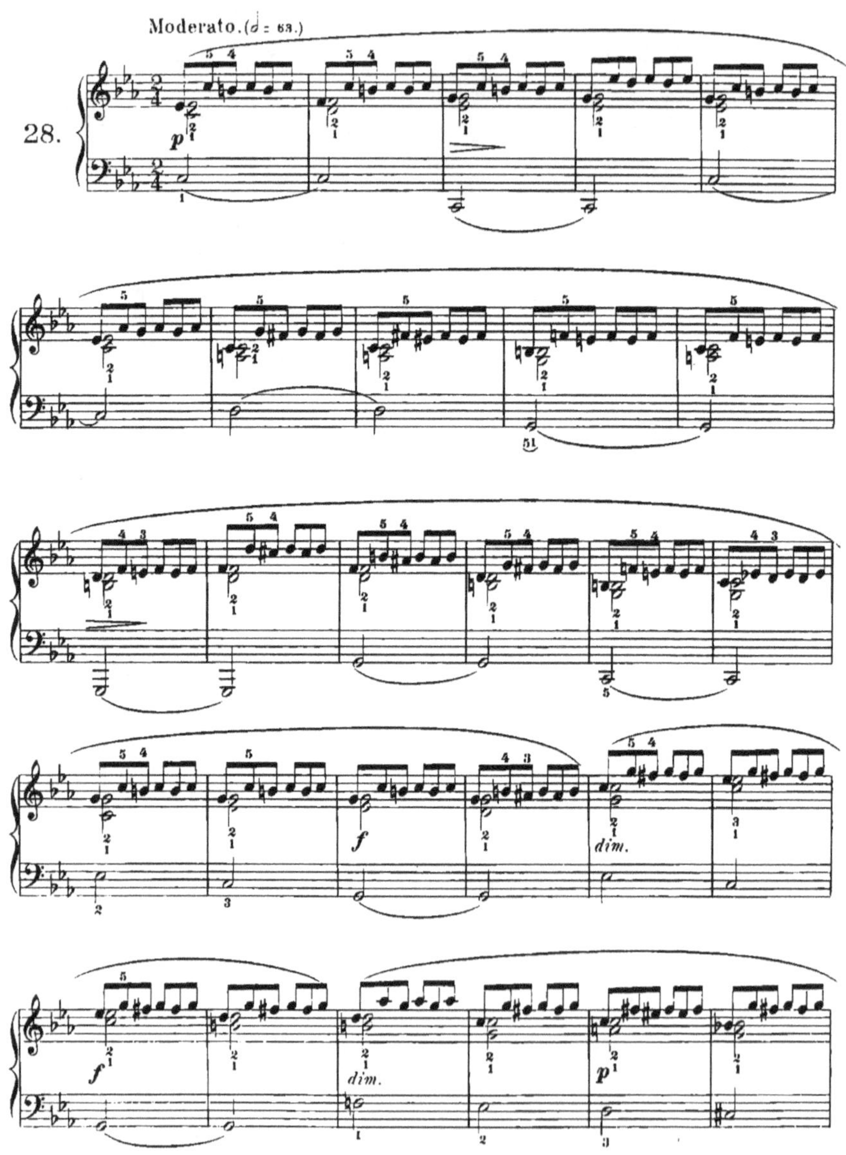
Moderato. (𝅗𝅥 = 63.)
28.
p
dim.
f
dim.
f
dim.
p

cresc.
dimin.
dolce.
cresc.
dimin.

Presto. (♩ = 132.)
simile
29.
mf
rf
f
p
dim.

cresc.

ff

rf

dimin.

rf

cresc.

51

f

p

f

p

ff

Moderato con espressione. (♩= 132.)

p
cresc.
p
cresc.
f
dim.
cresc.
f
dim.
p
pp

31.

Allegro. (♩= 92.)
p.
sempre stacc.
poco a poco cresc.
f
ff.
pp
dol.
cresc.
p
cresc.

f
dolce smorz.
p
poco a poco cresc.
ff
dim.
p
morendo.
pp

Più tosto presto. (♩. = 104)
32.

cresc.
dim.

Vivace. (♪= 100.)
33.
mezzo f

dimin.

dimin.

dimin.

Tempo agitato. (𝅗𝅥 = 116.)
34.
sf
cresc.
cresc.
f
p

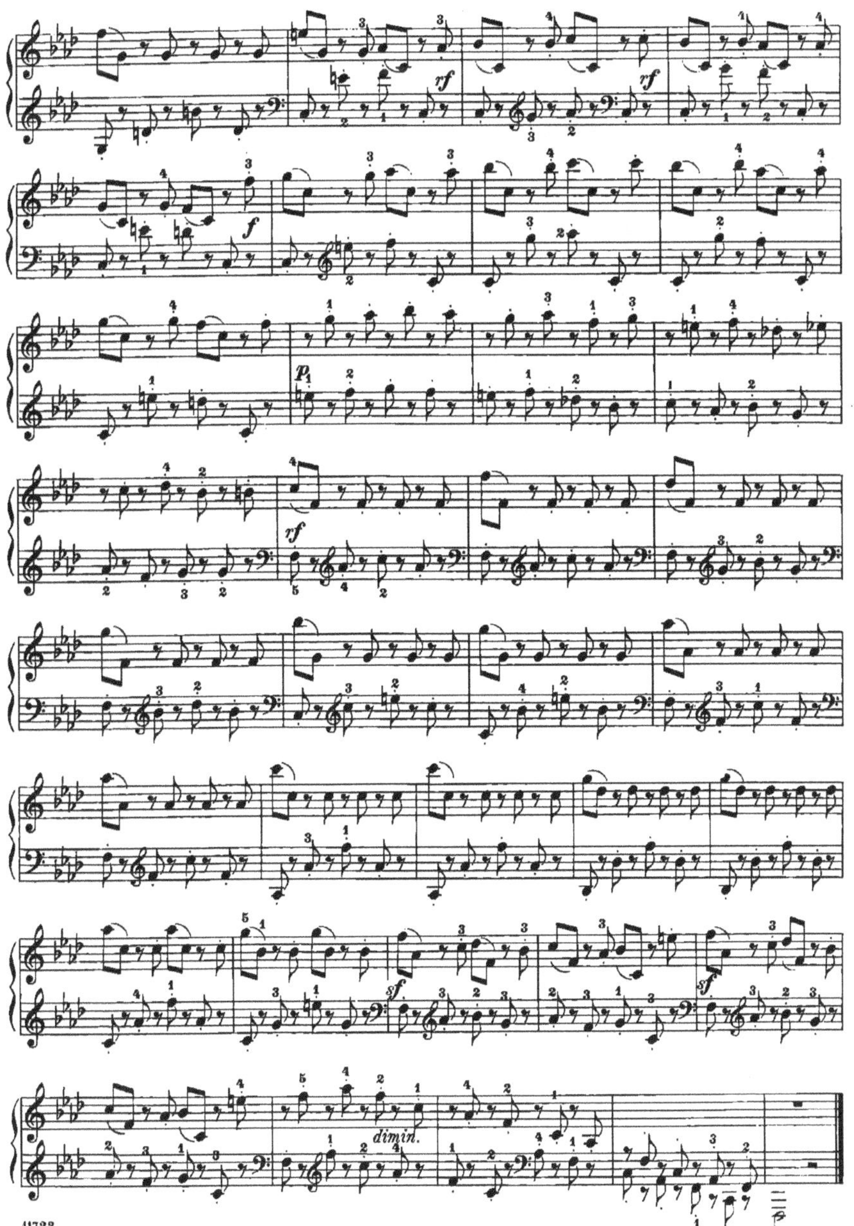

rf
rf
f
p
rf
sf
sf
dimin.

35.
Moderato. (♩ = 108)
rf
rf

rf
rf
cre
scen
do.
f

Allegro agitato. (♩. = 66.)
36.
dim.
dim.
dim.
cresc.

dimin.
p
cresc.
fz
f
dimin.
cre - scen - do.
f
dim.

Prestissimo. (𝅗𝅥 = 76)
37.
mf
ff
p

f

mf

dolce.

Moderato. (♩. = 88)
38.
dimin.
cresc.
p
ff
dimin.
p
rf

p
rf
dimin.
pp

Spiritoso assai. (𝅗𝅥 = 96.)
39.
rf
dimin.
f
ff

dolce.

Allegro comodo. (♪ = 126.)
40.
dimin.

f

dim.

fz

dim.

Aria.

Moderato. (♩. = 116.)

dolce

Allegro moderato, ma energico. (♩ = 138.)

42.

simile

p

poco a poco cresc.

ff con fuoco

ff

dimin.

f

dimin.
sf
mf
ff
8
dimin.
pp

www.ingramcontent.com/pod-product-compliance
Lightning Source LLC
Chambersburg PA
CBHW021442090426
42739CB00009B/1597
9783744783637